This book
belongs to:

Casey Thomas

This book
belongs to:

Casey Thomas

Dinosaurs

A LEARN TO READ BOOK

By Donald Silver
Illustrated by Patricia J. Wynne

CHECKERBOARD PRESS
NEW YORK

Copyright © 1989 Checkerboard Press, a division of Macmillan, Inc. All rights reserved.
ISBN 002-898254-1 Printed in U.S.A. Library of Congress Catalog Card Number: 89-646

CHECKERBOARD PRESS and colophon, BIG & EASY and elephant logo, are trademarks of Macmillan, Inc.

0 9 8 7 6 5 4 3 2 1

Stegosaurus

Dinosaurs lived long ago.

Apatosaurus

Brachiosaurus

The world was different then.

Brachiosaurus

Many dinosaurs were huge.

Saltopus

Some were as small as chickens.

Brachiosaurus

Albertosaurus

Triceratops

Ankylosaurus

Some dinosaurs had long necks.
Some had horns.

All dinosaurs were reptiles.

Many dinosaurs ate plants.

Parasaurolophus

Tyrannosaurus

Others were hunters. They ate meat.

The hunters had sharp teeth and claws.

Tenontosaurus

Deinonychus

Stegosaurus

Ankylosaurus

But many dinosaurs were difficult to kill.

Most dinosaurs laid eggs.

Maiasaura

Many eggs were eaten by other dinosaurs.

Oviraptor

Stenonychosaurus

Most baby dinosaurs were left on their own.

But some mothers took care of their babies.

Triceratops

Edmontosaurus

No one knows why all the dinosaurs died.

Dinosaur bones and fossils help people learn about dinosaurs.